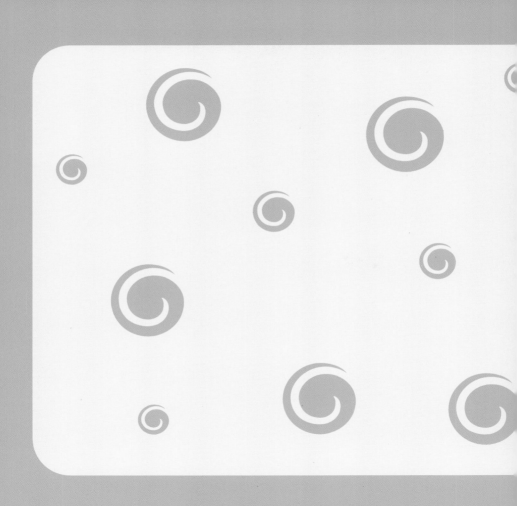

Eat Your Way To A

GREAT
BODY

LAGOON
BOOKS

Project Editor: Sylvia Goulding
Book Design: Norma Martin

Thanks to: Ann Marangos, Nick Daws, Jeremy Hemming and Geeta Naryanon

Series Editor: Lucy Dear
Managing Editor: Sarah Wells
Based on an original concept by Simon Melhuish

Published by:
LAGOON BOOKS
PO BOX 311, KT2 5QW, UK
PO BOX 990676, Boston, MA 02199 USA

ISBN: 1902813790

Printed in Hong Kong

The nutritional statements in this book are intended for your information only. Many of the claims made by nutritionists require further evaluation. Do not use to self-diagnose, treat, cure, or prevent disease, but instead seek information from qualified health-care practitioners.

Eat Your Way To A

GREAT
BODY

Introduction

Be honest. Is your body no longer a temple to health and fitness? Are your muscles flabby, eyes dull, hair lost its luster? Well, don't worry – help is at hand!

You don't have to suffer in the quest for a fabulous body. No need to fork out for expensive gym membership and spend hour upon hour pumping iron. The solution is much closer to home – in your own kitchen, in fact.

The plain truth is, to build a fabulous body you need fabulous food – and this book has all the recipes required. Here's just a taste of the lip-smacking, eye-brightening, body-boosting delights you'll find in the pages that follow…

A Trim Figure

Banish flabby flesh with the marvelous meals in Chapter One. From Lithe Lentil Soup to Thigh-Firming Enchiladas, Slimming Salmon Cakes to Young-Forever Curry, they'll put a spring in your step and a song in your heart.

A Sexy Body

One good reason for wanting a fabulous body is to attract others for fun and romance. From Seafood Maximizer to Work-Out Banana Cheesecake,

he tasty tempters in this
hapter will ensure you've got
t, so you can flaunt it!

ouch Me, Feel Me

ive your skin a healthy glow
vith the radiant recipes in
hapter Three. From Vitality
enison to Anti-Wrinkle
almon, Creamy Soft
lackberries to Peachy Skin
essert, these satin-smooth
epasts will give you a
omplexion to die for.

ere's Looking at You, Kid

ook and feel a million dollars
vith these inspiring and
nvigorating meals. From
ustrous Paprika Chicken to
Midnight Melon Soup, they'll
ensure you walk tall and
confident, and the rest of the
world sits up and begs.

It's true! Build these mouth-
watering meals into your daily
routine, and soon your body
will be humming like a finely-
tuned machine. With your
super-fit physique, you'll turn
heads wherever you go – and
be ready to face any challenge,
from white-water rafting down
the Amazon to a hot date with
the cutie of your dreams! So
why wait any longer? Turn the
page and start cooking. Your
fabulous body will soon be
ready to go!

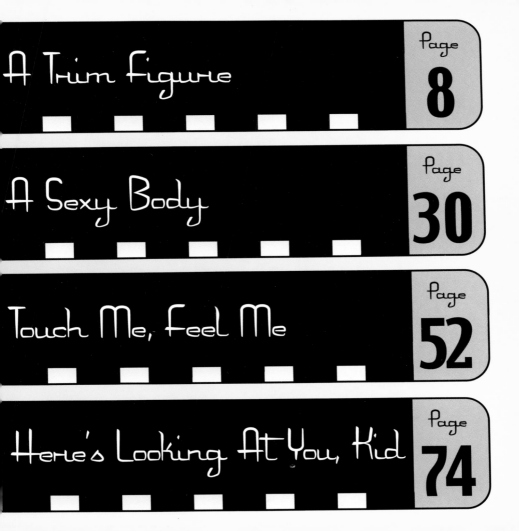

1

A Trim Figure

A healthy body is a great body – so get in tip-top shape now!

Contents

Rapid Rabbit Fricassée

For every pound of muscle you develop, your body burns a massive 35 calories. What easier way then to get into a trim shape? Just build up muscle with exercise and lean protein such as this French rabbit dish.

Serves 4

- 50 g/2 oz butter
- 1 tbs olive oil
- 1 onion, finely chopped
- 4 large rabbit joints
- 2 tsp flour
- 2 tbs mixed fresh herbs
- 285 ml/1/2 pint red wine
- 200 ml/7 fl oz chicken stock
- Salt and pepper

1 In a large pan, heat the butter and the oil. Fry the onion for 5 minutes. Add the rabbit, sprinkle over the flour and fry for 10 minutes, turning until evenly browned.

2 Chop the herbs. Add with the wine and stock, and season generously. Cover, and simmer for 30–40 minutes, until tender. Lift rabbit out, set aside and keep warm.

3 Boil the sauce uncovered for 3–5 minutes to reduce a little. Stir well to combine. Return the rabbit to the pan and heat through. Serve with boiled potatoes or rice.

Weightlifters' Sardine Quiche

Can't lift the shopping bag, or even less the sports bag to go to the gym? Transform yourself magically from couch potato to muscle man or woman. Increase your muscle power with this tasty fish dish.

Serves 4

- 225 g/8 oz plain (all-purpose) flour
- A pinch of salt
- 100 g/4 oz cold butter, cut into small pieces
- 250 g canned sardine, drained
- 75 g big onions, sliced thinly
- 1 tbsp chopped garlic
- 1½ tbsp curry powder
- 2 eggs
- ½ pint of hot milk
- 50 g/2 oz grated cheese
- Salt and pepper
- 1 beefsteak tomato, sliced
- 1 tsp paprika

1 Grease a 20 cm (8 in) quiche pan, line with grease-proof paper. Sift flour and salt into a bowl. With fingers, rub in the butter until crumbly. Stir in just enough ice-cold water to bind, and knead lightly. Cover and chill for 20–30 minutes.

2 Roll out the dough to fit the quiche pan. Trim the edges and prick the base with a fork. Chill for 20–30 minutes.

3 Heat oven to 200°C/400°F/ Gas 6. Line pastry with baking paper and baking beans; bake for 10 minutes. Reduce heat to 170°C/325°F/ Gas 3, remove paper and beans, bake for 5–10 minutes.

4 Heat 2 tbs oil, fry onion, garlic and curry powder for 5 minutes. Drain sardines, flake, and add. Leave to cool slightly.

5 Beat eggs and hot milk. Stir in cheese and melt. Season, add to sardines, pour into pastry shell.

6 Place tomato on top, and sprinkle with paprika. Bake for 30–40 minutes until golden. Serve hot or cold.

Muscling in

If your body is deficient in calcium, your muscles will be tense and stiff. To give you flab-free, strong and healthy legs and arms, treat yourself to fish. Eating calcium-rich food will make your muscles work properly and as an added bonus, it'll also bring relief if you're suffering from PMS.

Never eat more than you can lift...
(Miss Piggy)

Lithe Lentil Soup

Get the basic frame — your skeleton — in good working order so you can build on it. You need strong bones to support your muscles, and this lentil dish from Germany will help you form them.

<u>Serves 4</u>

- 1 tbs olive oil
- 2 slices bacon, cut into small pieces
- 1 onion, chopped
- 1 garlic clove, crushed
- 1 carrot, chopped
- 1 stick celery, chopped
- 1 tbs plain (all-purpose) flour
- Salt and pepper
- 1 bay leaf
- 150 g/5 oz brown lentils
- 1.2 liter/2 pints/5 cups beef or vegetable stock

- 1/2 tsp fresh thyme
- A pinch of ground nutmeg
- 1 potato, diced
- 1 tbs wine vinegar (optional)

1 Heat the oil in a large pan. Add bacon, onion, garlic, carrot, and celery, and fry gently for 5 minutes, or until the bacon is crisp. Stir in flour.

2 Pour in the stock and stir. Add the bay leaf, lentils, thyme, nutmeg, and potato, and season generously. Bring to a boil, reduce the heat, cover,

and simmer for 2 hours, or until the lentils are tender. Stir in the vinegar, if liked.

3 Serve with crusty sourdough bread and a glass of beer.

Though we travel the world over to find the beautiful, we must carry it with us or we find it not...
(Ralph Waldo Emerson)

Keep your finger on the pulses

Research in Finland has shown that men taking vitamin D supplements were 25 per cent less likely to suffer broken bones. Vitamin D – plentiful in pulses – will also give you an unblemished skin and clear, sparkly eyes.

Dem bones, dem bones...

Keep your bones and joints strong with weights and exercise. Lifting and carrying can also strengthen your bones: bend at the knees, keeping your upper body upright, to lift a weight, carry bags or young children on your back.

Svelte-Figure Roast Vegetables

If your waistline is bulging in an unsightly 'apple' shape, change your diet. Stick to as much fresh and unprocessed food as you can – your tummy will thank you.

Serves 4

- 2 aubergines (eggplants)
- 2 red (bell) peppers
- 4 small courgettes (zucchini)
- 1 head garlic
- 3 tbs olive oil
- Salt and pepper
- 1 tsp each chopped fresh thyme and rosemary
- 1 handful pine kernels
- 150 ml/4 fl oz plain yogurt
- A few sprigs fresh mint

1 Heat oven to 200°C/400°F/ Gas 6. Dice the aubergine (eggplant). Halve and de-seed (bell) peppers. Trim courgettes (zucchini) and cut into diagonal lengths. Separate the garlic into individual cloves without peeling them.

2 Place all the vegetables on an oiled baking tray, brush with oil, season generously, and sprinkle with the herbs. Roast

for about 30 minutes until the vegetables are beginning to change color but are still deliciously crunchy.

3 Dry-fry the pine kernels in a small pan, stirring, until golden. Sprinkle over the roasted vegetables. Transfer the yogurt to a small bowl. Chop the mint and stir in. Serve with the yogurt and pitta (flat) breads, or with a hot sauce. The vegetables also go well with sausages or grilled meat.

She not only kept her lovely figure, she's added so much to it...
(Bob Fosse)

A weight off your waist

Don't burden your stomach. Processed foods contain large amounts of saturated fats, sugars, emulsifiers, preservatives, colorings and flavorings. Cook your food from fresh ingredients and watch your waistline dwindle.

Number crunching

Lie flat on your back, knees bent and feet on the floor, arms folded behind your head. Slowly raise head and arms and lift your knees towards your elbows, curling your back and lifting your hips off the floor. Hold and count to five. Repeat.

Thigh-firming Enchiladas

We all hate the orange-peel effect of cellulite. You can combat cellulite with your diet and exercise, without resorting to expensive - and useless - creams.

Serves 4

- 2 sweet potatoes or yams
- 1 tbs oil
- 1 large onion, chopped
- 4 garlic cloves, crushed
- 5 chilies, de-seeded and diced
- 400 g/ 14 oz can black or other beans, drained
- 1 tsp ground cumin
- 1 tsp ground coriander
- 1 tsp chili powder
- 8 corn tortillas
- 2 tbs grated Monterey or Cheddar cheese

1 Peel and par-boil the sweet potatoes or yams in a large pan of boiling salted water for 5 minutes. Drain and dice.

2 Heat 1 tbs oil in a frying pan, add onion and fry for 3 minutes; add garlic and chilies, and cook for 2 minutes.

3 Add the spices and cook for 1 minute, stirring. Add the beans and cook for 10–15 minutes, or until a thick purée.

4 Heat the tortillas in a dry frying pan. Heat the grill to high. Spoon the bean-filling onto the center of the tortillas, and roll. Seal the inside edge with the filling, and place seam-side down on the tray. Sprinkle with cheese and cook for 5 minutes, until melted. Serve with guacamole.

The beauty that addresses itself to the eyes is only the spell of the moment – the eye of the body is not always that of the soul...
(George Sand)

Combat cellulite

There is some evidence that orange-peel, or cellulite, may be linked to chromium or nickel deficiency – cheese is rich in chromium and beans in nickel.

Brush yourself

Brush your skin swiftly once a day all over. Use a soft bristle brush and move to harder bristles. Brush in quick strokes, towards the heart, to remove excess water and improve circulation.

Spaghetti Carb-onara

To build strong muscle and avoid unsightly flabbiness, you need to exercise – there's no ways around it. However, your body will also need a plentiful supply of calories from unrefined, non-sugar carbs to build strong muscles, and these are plentiful in pasta dishes.

Serves 2

- 225 g/8 oz fresh spaghetti
- 1 garlic clove
- 2 eggs
- 2 tbs freshly grated Parmesan cheese
- Salt and pepper
- 4 slices bacon, diced
- 1 tsp olive oil

1 Heat the oil, add bacon and garlic, and fry for 5 minutes, or until browned. Meanwhile, whisk the eggs together in a jug and season with a little salt and plenty of pepper.

2 Cook the spaghetti in a large saucepan of salted boiling water for 3–5 minute, until al dente. Drain well.

3 Tip spaghetti into the pan with the bacon, stir in the eggs and half the Parmesan. The cheese should melt, and the eggs should half-set when in contact with the pasta. Serve immediately, with remaining Parmesan in a separate bowl to sprinkle on top.

Beauty is the adjustment
of all parts
proportionately so
that one cannot
add or subtract
or change
without
impairing the
harmony of the
whole...
(Leon B. Alberti)

Toning tactics

For toned arms and legs, build up
muscle through weight training,
and burn calories with cardio-
vascular exercise. Train with
weights three times a week, and
do aerobic exercises 3–5 times a
week, for 30 minutes. Walking
or running, rowing and cycling
are great to firm your body.

Perfect elbows

Eat a grapefruit, then rest your
elbows in the empty shells
for 10 minutes a day for
smooth and tight skin, and
enjoy the benefits of plenty
of vitamin C.

Shape-Changer Pumpkin Soup

If you put on weight easily, change to a low-fat diet, and increase your intake of calcium. Try this deliciously low-fat pumpkin soup for a start, and watch your shape improve!

Serves 4

- 1 tbs oil
- 1 onion, chopped
- 1-2 garlic cloves, crushed
- 1 tsp mild curry powder
- 1 large potato, chopped
- 900 g/2 lbs pumpkin, diced
- 225 g/8 oz carrots, diced
- 1.2 l/2 pints/5 cups vegetable stock
- 1 bay leaf
- Salt and pepper
- 150 ml/1/4 pint/ 5 fl oz semi-skimmed milk
- 2 tsp chopped fresh parsley

1 Heat the oil in a saucepan and fry the onion for 3 minutes; add the garlic and fry for 2 minutes, or until both are soft. Add the curry powder and fry for 1 minute, stirring.

2 Add the potato, pumpkin, and carrots, and gently fry for 2–3 minutes, stirring. Pour in the stock and the bay leaf, season to taste, stir, cover, and simmer gently for 20–30 minutes, or until the vegetables are tender.

3 Leave to cool a little, then purée with a hand-held

blender. Stir in the milk and reheat without bringing back to the boil. Sprinkle with the herbs and serve, with crusty slices of baguette.

Perfection is achieved, not when there is nothing more to add, but when there is nothing left to take away...
(Antoine de Saint Exupéry)

Pumpkin Calcium

Apart from eating less, especially less fat, and exercising more, try increasing your calcium intake, for example with calcium-rich pumpkin. Research at the University of Tennessee has shown that the amount of fat produced by the body is inversely proportional to the amount of calcium in the diet.

Flex your tum

Keep your tum supple: stand straight and twist sideways, back and forth, as far as you can, for 1 minute three times a day.

Slimming Salmon Cakes

Aiming for a trimmer, leaner self? Don't cut out all the fats in your diet – fat is an essential building block – just reduce the amount you eat, and opt for healthy seafood, which contains the healthiest fats!

Serves 4

- 450 g/1 lb salmon fillet, cut into chunks
- 50 g/2 oz breadcrumbs
- 1 onion, finely chopped
- 1 egg
- 1 tsp chopped fresh coriander leaves (cilantro)
- Salt and pepper
- ½ unwaxed lime (if not available unwaxed, scrub under hot water)
- 2 tbs olive oil

1 Blitz the fish in the blender, and put into a large bowl. Add the breadcrumbs together with the onion, egg, and coriander leaves (cilantro). Mix well to combine. Season to taste, and mix in the grated zest and juice of the lime.

2 Shape the mixture into small fishcakes. Add more breadcrumbs if the mixture is too sloppy to hold shape.

3 Heat the oil in a large frying pan. Fry the fishcakes in batches, for about 5 minutes each side, or until golden

brown. Pat dry with kitchen paper and serve immediately, with a baked potato.

You p*** me off you Salmon... You're too expensive in restaurants... (Eddie Izzard)

Sea food – and eat it

Australian researchers have shown that omega-3-rich salmon can help you reduce weight and improve your overall health. Participants in the study lost weight, lowered their LDL cholesterol levels, and reduced the risk of developing diabetes too. So get fishing now!

Get active

Walk or cycle rather than drive whenever possible. Park further away from your destination or get off the bus one stop earlier and walk the rest of the way.

Glowing Clam Chowder

Beauty in a casserole – this clam dish will help you shed the pounds and pile on the muscles – or should that be mussels?

Serves 4

- 600 ml/1 pint/2½ cups fish stock
- 450 g/1 lb waxy potatoes, diced
- 2 tbs butter
- 3 slices bacon, chopped
- 1 large onion, chopped
- 2 stalks celery, chopped
- 2 garlic cloves, chopped
- 1 bay leaf
- 100 g/4 oz plain (all-purpose) flour
- 1.5 kg /3½ lbs canned clams, drained, juices reserved
- 300 ml/10 fl oz/1 ¼ cups single (light) cream
- 1 tsp hot pepper sauce

1 In a large saucepan bring the fish stock to the boil. Add the potato cubes and bring back to boil. Reduce the heat, cover, and simmer gently for 3-4 minutes. Remove from the heat; do not drain.

2 Heat the butter in a large, heavy saucepan, add the bacon and cook for 5 minutes, or until it begins to brown. Add the onion, celery, garlic, and bay leaf, and cook for

about 3–5 minutes over a low heat, or until the vegetables are just beginning to soften. Stir in the flour and cook, stirring, for 2 minutes. Beat in the reserved clam juices, a little at a time.

3 Add the potatoes and fish stock, the clams, cream, and hot pepper sauce. Simmer the chowder for 10 minutes to blend the flavors, stirring frequently. Season to taste with salt and pepper, and serve, piping hot, with crusty bread.

Clamoring for clams

Clams are low in fat and calories, but high in iron, needed for the production of red blood cells, and in chromium picolinate. Studies have shown that increasing chromium levels in the diet markedly lowers body weight and fat, while increasing lean body mass. Just what we're after, then!

Snack attack

To energize yourself, nibble on nuts, raisins, dried fruit and seeds instead, to stave off hunger pangs, and give yourself a long-lasting energy injection.

Young-Forever Bean Curry

Can you feel the onset of middle-aged spread? Figure beginning to sag a little? Stay trim in figure and young in body longer with this deliciously spicy dish.

Serves 4

- 125 g/4 oz split skinless moong dhal or lima beans
- 2 tbs oil
- 1 tsp cumin seeds
- 1 onion, chopped
- 2 garlic cloves, crushed
- 1 piece fresh ginger, about 1 cm/½ in, peeled and finely chopped
- 2 tbs tomato purée
- 2 tbs flaked coconut
- 2 tbs fresh coriander leaves (cilantro), chopped
- ¼–1 tsp Cayenne pepper
- ½ tsp paprika
- Salt

1 Rinse the beans in fresh, cold water, place in a large bowl cover with cold water and leave to soak, or overnight. Drain and rinse again. Set aside.

2 Heat the oil in a large saucepan, add the cumin seeds, onion, and ginger. Fry for about 5 minutes, or until the onion starts to brown, add the garlic and cook for a further minute, stirring. Stir in the tomato purée, coconut, and reduce the heat and cook until the tomato is soft.

3 Stir in 2 tbs water, then purée the mixture with a hand-held blender until smooth. Add more water if necessary.

4 Add the beans, stir. Add 600 ml/1 pint/2½ cups water, stir, and bring to a boil. Reduce the heat, cover, and cook for 30-60 minutes, or until beans are tender, but have not yet disintegrated.

5 Stir in the Cayenne, paprika, and salt to taste. Add the coriander leaves (cilantro), and stir to mix thoroughly. Serve on a bed of whole-grain rice.

Miss India

If you feel like you're getting old before your time, and your body seems to be deteriorating, you may be deficient in molybdenum, silicon, or both. Deficiency in these elements can lead to premature aging – a decline in the skin's elasticity, osteoporosis, hardened arteries, and many more age-related evils. So dig into this curry and keep your youthful body intact for longer, as dried beans, lentils, whole-grain rice, and cereals are rich in both elements.

2

A Sexy Body

**Eat these tasty morsels
for an alluring physique**

Contents

High Fiber Chili Potatoes

Fiber fights flab. So, if you're after a svelte figure, try this high-fiber combo – easy to make and delicious too!

Serves 2

- 2 large baking potatoes
- 1 tbs oil
- 1 small onion, chopped
- 2 garlic cloves
- 5 chilies, chopped
- 1 tsp ground coriander seeds
- 1 tbs tomato purée
- 100 g/4 oz canned red kidney beans
- 100 g/4 oz canned chopped tomatoes

1 Heat oven to 200°C/400°F/ Gas 6. Spear the potatoes with a metal skewer and bake for about 1½ hours. Check with a sharp knife to see if they're done. Alternatively, microwave for 20 minutes.

2 Meanwhile make the chili sauce. Heat the oil in a saucepan, add onion, garlic, and chilies, and fry, stirring, for about 5 minutes or until softened. Stir in the coriander and tomato purée and cook for 1 minute, stirring. Add beans and tomatoes, stir to mix, and simmer for 20 minutes.

3 Serve the jacket potatoes with the chili beans. Do not add extra butter.

Mango Fool

Mango is a refreshingly tropical treat any time of day, and believe it or not, it will give your body the perfect holiday sun protection too.

Serves 4

- 1 fresh mango
- 2 tbs sugar
- 250 ml/9 fl oz double (heavy) cream

1 Over a bowl, cut top and bottom 'lids' off the mango, catching all the juices, then slice down either side of the flat stone. Cut the flesh from the peel, and blitz in a food processor. Push purée through a fine sieve and stir in the sugar.

2 In a separate bowl, whip the cream until it forms stiff peaks. Fold into the mango. Serve immediately or chill in the fridge for up to 4 hours.

Mango Skin Smoothie

Serves 4

- 1 mango
- 1 banana
- 2 tsp honey
- Crushed ice
- 425 ml/3/4 pint/2 cups low-fat milk
- 175 ml/6 fl oz single (light) cream or yogurt

1 Carefully peel the mango, catching all the juices over a bowl. Peel the banana.

2 Whizz mango, banana and all other ingredients in a blender. Pour into chilled glasses and serve.

Appealing without peeling

Get a healthy, natural tan and protect your skin. Mangoes – like carrots, spinach and cantaloupe melons – are rich sources of beta-carotene, which reduces the risk of sunburn (unattractive and dangerous!) and delays aging.

Sex appeal is 50 per cent what you've got and 50 per cent what people think you've got... (Sophia Loren)

Mushroom & Beef Muscle Builder

If you're after a rippled, rock-hard stomach, try this lip-smacking gratin. Combine its figure-enhancing properties with tummy-toning exercises for max effect.

Serves 4

- 1 garlic clove, crushed
- 1 tsp fresh thyme, chopped
- 2 tbs oil
- Salt and pepper
- 450 g/1 lb fillet of beef, cut into thin strips
- 225 g/8 oz breadcrumbs
- 1 large red onion, chopped
- 1 bunch parsley, chopped
- 2 tbs tomato purée
- 2 beef tomatoes, sliced
- 225 g/8 oz mushrooms
- 100 g/4 oz single (light) cream
- 1 tbs Dijon mustard

1 In a bowl, stir together garlic, thyme, and oil; season. Place beef in the marinade, stir to coat, and chill for 30 minutes.

2 Meanwhile, combine breadcrumbs, onion, parsley, and tomato purée, and season.

3 Heat oven to 200°C/400°F/ Gas 6. Put the meat and marinade into a large frying pan. Fry, stirring, for 1 minute, or until the meat has taken on color. Transfer to an ovenproof dish. Fry

mushrooms in the same pan
for 2 minutes, stirring, add
cream and mustard. Stir, then
combine with the beef.

4 Spread the breadcrumb
mixture over the beef and
mushrooms, lay the tomato
slices on top, and bake for
about 10–20 minutes, or until
a golden crust has formed.
Serve immediately.

love the male
body, it's better designed
than the male mind...
(Andrea Newman)

Ab fab abs

Mushrooms are power parcels of
chromium picolinate, which the
body uses to control blood sugar.
It reduces body fats and builds up
muscle if combined with exercise.
So book a session at the gym.

Taut Tum!

For washboard abs, lie on
your back, legs on the
seat of a chair. Fold
arms across chest.
Slowly lift shoulders,
neck, and head off the
floor and touch your
knees with your elbows.

Seafood Maximizer

Girls! Get yourselves a cleavage to be proud of with this delicious seafood dish!

Serves 4

- 1 tbs oil
- 2 garlic cloves, crushed
- A piece of ginger, about 2½ cm/1 in, finely chopped
- 1 chili, chopped
- 225 g/8 oz fresh mixed shellfish (crabmeat, mussels, scallops or squid)
- 225 g/8oz fresh peeled prawns (shrimps)
- 1 bunch spring onions (scallions), chopped diagonally
- 1 red (bell) pepper, de-seeded and cut into strips
- 125 g/4 oz canned beansprouts, drained
- 125 g/4 oz mangetouts (snow peas)
- 2 tbs soy sauce
- ½ tsp Chinese five spice
- 1-2 tbs sherry

1 Heat oil in a large frying pan or wok, add garlic, ginger, and chili, and fry over a high heat, stirring, for 1 minute.

2 Add the onions (scallions) and (bell) pepper, and continue frying for 2 minutes, stirring all the time. Add the mixed shellfish and the prawns (shrimps), and continue frying for about 3 minutes, stirring all the time.

3 Add the beansprouts and mangetout (snow peas). Stir in the soy sauce, spice, and sherry, and continue frying for about 2 minutes, stirring all the time.

4 Serve with egg-fried rice and a cup of hot green tea.

...improve my bust. Push-ups are one of the best exercises for perfect breasts. Start with just five, then increase the number of press-ups in groups of five as you get warmed up.
Other good breast-ercises: canoeing, swimming and rock-climbing.

I do wish my breasts were bigger. Not big... but less small...
(Calista Flockhart)

Potent Pea Soup

Enjoy this summery soup from the Emerald Isle, which will do wonders for your body's performance rating!

Serves 4

- 900 ml/1 1/2 pints/30 fl oz ham or vegetable stock
- 225 g/8 oz fresh green peas, shelled, pods reserved
- 25 g/1 oz butter
- 2 slices rindless bacon, chopped
- 1 onion, chopped
- 1 small head lettuce, shredded
- 1 tsp chopped mint, plus whole leaves for the garnish
- 1 tsp chopped fresh parsley
- Salt and pepper
- 1 tsp sugar
- 1 tbs single (light) cream

1 Heat the stock in a large saucepan. Add the peas and bring back to the boil.

2 Meanwhile, heat the butter in a frying pan, fry bacon and onion for 5 minutes. Add the lettuce and herbs, and fry for 2 minutes, stirring all the time.

3 Tip the lettuce mixture into the saucepan with the peas and season. Add the sugar and stir.

4 Bring back to the boil, reduce the heat, cover, and simmer, stirring occasionally, for 30 minutes, or until the peas are soft. Whizz with a puréeing stick if you prefer.

5 Transfer the soup to four individual soup bowls, swirl a little cream into each serving and garnish with the reserved whole mint leaves.

There's nothing better than good sex. But bad sex? A peanut butter and jelly sandwich is better than bad sex...
(Billy Joel)

Pulse-racing stuff!

What use is a fabulous body if you can't perform in the bedroom? Make sure your potency potential is second to none by including plenty of zinc, vitamins B and E, and especially molybdenum in your diet. Processed foods have mostly had their molybdenum-rich shells stripped out. Don't miss out on this potency element in your diet – eat unprocessed grains, nuts, seeds and pulses, raw fruit and vegetables, eggs, and drink fresh fruit juice.

41

Fabulous Legs Salad Lunch

This low-carb lunch combined with targeted exercise will help you shed pounds and give you perfect pins for the summer. So unpack those hot pants now.

Serves 4

- 450 g/1 lb baby leaf spinach
- 4 baby goats' cheeses
- 8 radishes, sliced
- 8 sun-dried tomatoes in oil, drained and sliced
- 2 tbs olive oil
- 1 tbs balsamic vinegar

1 Heat the grill to high. Carefully wash and shred the spinach leaves, removing any hard stems and yellow leaves. Distribute the spinach onto four serving plates.

2 Slice the goats' cheeses, brush with a little olive oil and place on a baking tray. Grill for about 5 minutes, or until the slices have turned a golden color.

3 Place the cheese slices in the center of each plate, and then arrange the sliced radishes and sun-dried tomatoes around the outside. Drizzle with oil and vinegar. Serve with a glass of mineral water. Very refreshing!

There are two reasons why I'm in show business, and I'm standing on both of them... (Betty Grable)

Low-carb legs

Low-carb diets work on the principle that you can eat what you want as long as you avoid heavily processed high-carb foods such as sugar, white flour and breads. On this diet, weight loss is generally proportional to the exclusion of carbohydrates.

Seaside frolic

A great way to tone your thighs is to run along the beach in hip-high water. The water's resistance will work off the flab and get your heart and circulation going too. So grab that frisbee now.

Perfect Buns Lamb Pockets

Is your rear view turning the heads of the guys at the building site – or the girls in the office – as you walk past? If not, perk up your seat cushion with these powerful protein pockets.

Serves 4

- 225 g/8 oz plain low-fat yogurt
- 1/4 cucumber
- 2 1/2 onions
- 3 garlic cloves, crushed
- A pinch of sugar
- 450 g/1 lb lean ground lamb
- 1 tsp ground coriander seeds
- 1 tsp ground cumin seeds
- 1 tbs paprika
- 1 egg
- Salt and pepper
- Breadcrumbs, if needed
- 1 tbs olive oil
- 4 whole-meal pitta pocket breads
- 2 tomatoes, sliced

1 To make the sauce, put the yogurt into a bowl. Peel, deseed and grate the cucumber; finely chop 1/2 onion; add both to the bowl. Stir in a third of the garlic and the sugar; mix well to combine. Cover and chill until ready to eat.

2 In a large mixing bowl, combine the lamb, remaining garlic, coriander, cumin, and paprika. Crack in the egg.

Finely chop 1 onion and add. Season to taste. Knead and shape into small, flat burgers. If the mixture is too sloppy, add more breadcrumbs.

3 Heat the oil in a large frying pan. Add the burgers, in batches if necessary, and fry for about 5 minutes each side, or until cooked all the way through (check by cutting into one).

4 Meanwhile heat the pitta pockets and open them out; thinly slice the remaining onion. Fill the pittas with the burgers, tomato and onion slices, and yogurt sauce, and serve immediately.

Pinky and perky _ _ _ _ _ _ _

If you no longer fit into your favorite chair, you probably need to lose weight, but this can leave your derrière looking flat, saggy, and sad. Make sure you train your muscles and eat low-fat protein such as this lamb dish to improve muscle structure for a sexy butt.

Running up the hill..._

Walk or run up a sand dune – the sand will give way, making it harder. It'll shape your calves and do wonders for your gluteals.

Work-Out Banana Cheesecake

Exercise is the best way to better health and a trim figure. So work that body – and here's a scrumptious piece of cake to give you the energy to sustain your regime.

Makes 1 cake

- 175 g /6 oz digestive wholemeal biscuits
- 50 g/2 oz butter
- 450 g/1 lb low-fat cream cheese
- 75 g/3 oz sugar
- 1 ripe banana
- 2 eggs
- 25 g/1 oz chopped almonds
- 2 tbsp orange liquor
- Chocolate chips

1 Heat the oven to 180°C/ 350°F/Gas 4. Crush the biscuits to fine crumbs with a rolling pin and put into a bowl. Melt the butter and stir into the crumbs. Line a 23 cm/9 in greased loose-bottomed flan tin with the crumbs.

2 Place the cream cheese, sugar, and banana into a large bowl, and whizz with a hand-held mixer until you have a smooth purée.

3 Add the eggs, one at a time, mixing well after each addition. Stir in the almonds and the liquor, then pour the

Beauty is eternity gazing at itself in a mirror... (Kahlil Gibran)

banana mixture onto the crust and distribute evenly. Bake for 45 minutes.

4 Remove the tin from the oven. Loosen the cake from the rim by running a pallet knife around it; leave the cake to cool a little before removing the rim.

5 Slide the cake off the tin base and leave to cool completely on a wire grid. Top with chocolate chips and serve – as soon as possible!

Go bananas

Just one banana a day will give you sufficient energy to work out for 1 hour at the gym. What's more, it also stimulates the production of the feel-happy hormone serotonin, so you just can't lose: a trim and healthy body, and a big smile...

Wash and go

Make your hair happy too. Mash a banana, stir in 1 tbs grapeseed oil. Spread onto the ends of your hair, leave to set for 30 minutes. Rinse well and admire yourself.

Spring Bust-Buster Pasta

If you're looking to take your assets down a size or two, don't go on a crash diet which would do more harm than good. Reduce your measurements with this gorgeous low-fat, low-calorie spring dish.

Serves 4

- 100 g/4 oz broccoli florets
- 100 g/4 oz green beans
- 1 small fennel bulb
- 1 tbs olive oil
- 1 onion, finely chopped
- 3 garlic cloves, crushed
- 125 ml/4 fl oz/1/2 cup vegetable or chicken stock
- 100 g/4 oz fresh or frozen peas
- 2 tbs fresh herbs (rosemary, thyme, tarragon, parsley), finely chopped

- 450 g/1 lb rigatoni or penne
- 1 tbs single (light) cream
- Salt and pepper

1 Separate the broccoli florets into very small florets. Trim the beans and slice diagonally. Cut the base and hard outer leaves from the fennel; slice, and remove hard inner core.

2 In a large saucepan, heat the oil, add the onion and garlic, and cook for about 5 minutes, or until softened. Add the stock

and bring to the boil. Add the broccoli, beans, and fennel, bring back to the boil. Reduce heat, cover and simmer for 5 minutes, stirring, until just tender with a little crunch. Add peas and herbs, and cook for another 2 minutes.

3 Meanwhile, cook pasta in a large pan of salted boiling water following instructions, then drain. Stir the cream into the vegetables, season to taste, and serve with the pasta.

If I hadn't been a woman, I'd have been a drag queen... (Dolly Parton)

Does size matter?

Preferences for breast size have changed dramatically over the last few thousand years. Supermodels Twiggy and Kate Moss led the trend for smaller boobs, whilst Jane Russell and Marilyn Monroe gave you a real eyeful. The Venus of Willendorf, a prehistoric erotic statuette, however, would have measured a staggering 244 cm/96 in around the bust!

Tummy-Toner Chicken

A healthy digestion is vital for perfect looks. A rumbling or irritable stomach will make your tummy bloated. Try this soothing, low-fat chicken dish – and you'll soon look your best again.

Serves 4

- ■ 2 tbs oil
- ■ 8 small chicken pieces
- ■ 1 large onion, chopped
- ■ 425 ml/15 fl oz chicken stock
- ■ 3 sweet potatoes, peeled and sliced
- ■ 1/4 green cabbage, shredded
- ■ Salt and pepper
- ■ 1 tbs cornflour (cornstarch)

1 Heat half the oil in large frying pan. Add the chicken and fry for 10 minutes, or until browned all over. Remove and keep warm. Add the remaining oil and the onion, and fry for 5 minutes, stirring occasionally, until softened.

2 Return the chicken to the pan, add the stock, sweet potatoes, and cabbage, and season to taste. Bring to the boil, reduce heat, cover, and simmer for 30 minutes or until chicken and vegetables are done and tender, stirring occasionally.

The human body is
the best picture of the
human soul...
(Ludwig Wittgenstein)

3 In a small cup, combine the cornflour (cornstarch) with
2 fl oz water. Gradually stir
the mixture into the
casserole dish. Cook
and continue
cooking for
about 5 minutes,
or until the sauce
has thickened.
Serve on rice or
noodles.

Nervous tummy

Stress can make your stomach
cramp up, blocking essential
blood flow which makes you feel
and look bloated. Soothe away
the tension with easy-to-digest
chicken and stomach-calming
sweet potatoes.

Take on the world

Massage your body with a mint
or rosemary body lotion after
showering – both herbs are
therapeutic, boasting healing,
stimulating, and invigorating
properties. You'll feel revived,
ready to take on anything.

3

Touch me, feel me

Give your skin the velvet touch...

Contents

Caring Curried Carrots

One of the best things you can do for your skin is to treat yourself to this carrot dish, crammed with beta-carotene. It regulates skin moisture and fights free radicals that wreak havoc with your skin's elasticity. It'll also provide sunburn protection.

Serves 4

- 450 g/1 lb carrots, cut into fingers
- 1 tbs marmalade
- 2 tsp lemon juice
- 1 tsp Dijon mustard
- 1 tsp curry powder
- 1 tbs olive oil
- 2 tsp brown sugar
- 50 g/2 oz raisins

1 Place carrots in a steamer set over a pan of boiling water. Cover and steam for 3-5 minutes, or until tender. Remove and set aside.

2 In a small bowl, combine the marmalade, lemon juice, mustard, and curry powder. In a large nonstick pan, heat the oil. Add carrots, sugar, and raisins, and cook for about 2 minutes, stirring all the time.

3 Add the spice mixture, and cook for about 2 minutes, stirring constantly and scraping down sides of the pan. Serve the glazed carrots as a side dish with tender roast chicken.

Anti-Wrinkle Salmon

Did you know you had a facelift in the fridge? It's easy to look gorgeous – just dish up some sensational salmon with a delicious salsa verde, and take years off your face.

Serves 4

- 4 salmon steaks
- Salt and pepper
- 4 tbs olive oil plus oil for brushing
- 2 spring onions (scallions)
- 1 tbs chopped fresh coriander (cilantro) leaves

1 Heat the grill to high. Oil a large sheet of aluminium (aluminum) foil and place the salmon on top. Season to taste with salt and pepper, brush with a little oil, and place under the grill. Cook for 7-10 minutes on each side, or until the fish is done.

2 Meanwhile, heat 4 tbs oil in a small pan, add the spring onions (scallions), coriander (cilantro), and a pinch of salt. Cook for 2-3 minutes, or until the onion is softened, leave to cool a little, then blitz all the ingredients together in a blender until you have a smooth and green salsa.

3 Serve the salmon, drizzled with the green salsa, and boiled new potatoes.

Everything has beauty,
but not everyone sees it...
                    (Confucius)

Oil on flames

Salmon is rich in omega-3-fatty and eicosapentanoic acids, which are anti-inflammatory and quickly repair the damage done by free radicals. They're also effective against dry, flaky skin.

Oily skin

You wouldn't rub salmon on your skin, but why not try rosehip oil? Tests have shown that after three weeks of regular application. wrinkles started to disappear, spots to fade. After four months the skin was smooth and fresh.

Crinkle-Cure Crêpes

Banish that botox – here comes the easy and painless way to smooth skin. Just dish up a crêpe, and you'll be giving your skin a treat.

Serves 2

- 100 g/4 oz wholegrain (whole-wheat) flour
- 225 ml/8 fl oz/1 cup milk
- 2 eggs
- A pinch of salt
- 1 tbs oil
- 50 g/2oz ham, diced
- ½ tbs parsley, chopped

1 Heat oven to 150°C/300°F/ Gas 2. In a large bowl, beat together the flour and the milk with a hand-held blender. Beat in the eggs and the salt, until you have a smooth batter.

Cover and leave to stand in a warm place for about 1 hour.

2 Check the batter – it should still be liquid enough to close immediately after a wooden spoon has been pulled through the bowl. If necessary, add a little more milk. Stir in the chopped ham and parsley.

3 Heat the oil in a large non-stick frying pan. Add a couple of spoonfuls of the batter, and twist and turn the pan so that it covers the surface evenly. If any holes appear in the pancake as it sets, add a little more batter.

4 As soon as the underside of the crêpe is golden, use a fish slice to turn it over. Cook the other side for 1-2 minutes, then take the crêpe out of the pan, place on a hot serving plate, and keep warm in the oven until you have made crêpes from all the batter.

Egg-citing news

Eggs are a good source of vitamin A, which helps prevent dry skin, spots, and skin infections. Tests have shown that vitamin A banishes wrinkles – it does so by encouraging collagen production, causing the middle layers of the dermis to fill out and retain moisture more effectively.

The secret of staying young is to live honestly, eat slowly, and lie about your age... (Lucille Ball)

Nourishing Chicken and Salsa

A lean summery treat, packed with protein and vitamins, which you can also cook on the barbecue if the weather is right. And the salsa will give your skin all the extra nutrients it needs.

Serves 2

- 2 chicken breasts
- 1 tomato
- 1/2 onion
- 1 avocado
- 2 tbs fresh coriander leaves (cilantro)
- Juice of 1 lime or 1/2 lemon
- Salt and pepper
- A pinch of Cayenne pepper
- 2 tbs olive oil

1 Heat the grill to high. Skin the chicken breast and cut the flesh into 2.5 cm/1 in cubes. Halve, de-seed, and dice the tomato. Peel and chop the onion. Peel, stone, and dice the avocado. Chop the coriander leaves (cilantro).

2 Combine the vegetables in a bowl. Stir in the lime or lemon juice, coriander leaves (cilantro), and season to taste with salt, pepper, and Cayenne pepper.

3 Push the chicken pieces onto kebab (kabob) skewers, brush with olive oil and cook under the grill for about 10 minutes, turning occasionally,

until the chicken is cooked.
Serve with plain brown rice
and the avocado salsa.

Repair and rebuild

Avocado is rich in protein and contains large amounts of vitamin E, a vital antioxidant that slows down aging. It helps regenerate cells and improves skin elasticity.

Food in your face

Buy an extra avocado and mash the flesh with 1 tsp honey. Spread the paste over your face and leave for 10-15 minutes, then wash off. Your face will feel fresh, with taut skin, and well-nourished cells.

Smooth-Skin Seafood Pizza

Do you suffer from problem skin? Every time you have a date, does your skin let you down? It's time for a visit to the pizza parlor!

Serves 2

- 2 tbs olive oil
- 1 small onion, cut into very thin rings
- 2 garlic cloves, crushed
- 2 beef tomatoes, sliced
- Salt and pepper
- 2 pizza bases (23 cm/9 in or 30 cm/12 in diameter)
- 1 pack mixed seafood salad (including prawns [shrimps], mussels, squid rings)
- 1 tbs chopped fresh dill
- 1 tsp chopped fresh mint
- 4 tbs grated Parmesan, plus extra to serve

1 Heat oven to 180°C/350°F/ Gas 4. In a small frying pan, heat 1 tbs oil. Add the onion and garlic, and cook over a gentle heat until just turning color. Add the tomato slices and continue cooking over a low heat until the tomato has softened a little.

2 Spread the tomato-onion mixture over the pizza bases. Distribute the mixed seafood evenly over the top. Sprinkle with the chopped herbs, then drizzle with the remaining oil. Sprinkle the grated Parmesan over the top and bake in the

oven for 6-8 minutes, or until the cheese has melted. Serve with a green salad, and a glass of white wine.

Healing prawns

All seafood is packed with zinc which reduces skin inflammation, so it's perfectly soothing for all sufferers of acne, eczema, or psoriasis. Crumble some fresh Parmesan over the top, to get an extra dose of zinc.

When you are young, never smile – it causes wrinkles. But when you are old, smile all the time – it hides them...
(Marlene Dietrich)

Skin Treat Trout

This unusual Chinese dish uses tea leaves to give the fish a deliciously smoky aroma while providing your skin with great nutrients.

Serves 2

- 4 tbs jasmine tea leaves
- 4 tbs brown sugar
- 4 tbs long-grain rice
- 2 chunky trout fillets
- Salt and pepper
- 1 bunch watercress
- 1 tsp capers
- 1 garlic clove
- 1 tsp Dijon mustard
- 1 tbs lemon juice
- 4 tbs olive oil

1 Line a large frying pan or wok with two sheets of aluminium (aluminum) foil.

Combine the tea leaves, sugar, and rice, and put on top of the foil. Place a trivet on top and cover the wok or frying pan with a tight fitting lid. Place on a high heat for 6-8 minutes, or until a strong smoke develops.

2 Season the trout fillets. Remove the lid and place the trout on top of the trivet, with the skin side down. Cover again and cook for 5 minutes. Remove the pan from the heat, but leave to stand covered.

3 Meanwhile make the green salsa. In the blender, blitz watercress, capers, and garlic together with the mustard, lemon juice, and oil, until you have a thick green salsa.

4 Discard the tea leaves and rice. Serve the trout with boiled new potatoes, and the green salsa. Leftover salsa will keep in the fridge for a week.

Beauty tip

The essential oil of the tea tree plant is one of the most effective natural substances for killing or inhibiting the growth of bacteria, viruses, and fungi. It penetrates the skin and can be used to treat burns, scrapes, bites, stings, and skin irritations.

Tea-total

Make tea your ally in the anti-aging battle. The polyphenolic acid in tea helps your skin fight damage from pollution. So, instead of drinking alcohol, pour yourself a cup of green tea.

Vitality Venison

Venison is a deliciously lean meat that will give you plenty of minerals for a youthful complexion as well as healthy hair. It's also very low in fat and thus the perfect meal to keep that svelte figure.

Serves 2

- 1 unwaxed orange (if not available unwaxed, scrub under hot water)
- 150 g/5 oz fresh cranberries
- Sugar to taste
- 1 tbs olive oil
- 2 venison steaks
- Salt and pepper

1 Make the cranberry purée first. Cut the unpeeled orange into large chunks.

2 In a blender, quickly blitz the orange chunks together with the cranberries. Remove the purée, which should still have some structure, and place in a bowl. Stir in sugar to taste, to make the purée sweeter or more pungent. Set aside.

3 Heat the oil in a frying pan large enough to hold both of the steaks. Season the venison to taste with salt and pepper. Place the steaks in the pan, sear quickly for 1 minute on each side, then lower the heat.

4 Cook the steaks for about 3 minutes each side for a fairly rare steak, 5 minutes for medium and about 7-8 minutes for well done.

5 Serve the venison steaks with boiled new potatoes, green beans and carrots, and the cranberry purée.

Never purchase beauty products in a hardware store...
(Miss Piggy)

Metal guru

Lean red meat, such as venison, is a good source of iron. Many young women suffer from some iron deficiency and are slightly anemic. The iron in this dish will help prevent pale skin and loss of hair associated with anemia.

Happy faces

Smile! You'll reap the benefits in no time – you'll look younger and happier which will make you feel happier, and the people around you will feel much more positive towards you.

Creamy Soft Blackberries

A delightfully sensuous dessert to round off a healthy meal, and it'll leave your skin looking healthy and young!

Serves 2

- 225 g/8 oz blackberries
- 1 small unwaxed orange (if only available waxed, scrub well under hot water)
- 2 tbs caster (superfine sugar)
- 100 g/4 oz mascarpone (or other cream cheese)
- 50 g/2 oz plain yogurt
- A pinch of cinnamon

1 Pick over the blackberries; reserve about 50 g/2 oz of perfect whole fruits for the decoration. Put the remaining berries into a bowl and mash lightly with a fork.

2 In a second bowl, grate the zest of the orange and squeeze out the juice. Stir in the sugar, mascarpone, and yogurt, stirring well to combine. Sprinkle over a little cinnamon to taste.

3 Fold the mashed berries into the creamy mixture. Place some of the reserved berries into dessert glasses, spoon the cream on top, then decorate with the remaining whole berries. Chill until serving – if you can wait that long.

Beauty is truth, truth is beauty, that is all... and all you need to know...
(John Keats)

Skin savior

Blackberries are packed with vitamins C and E. C keeps your skin oily, elastic, and resilient, while E prevents premature aging and skin cancer. The berries also protect against environmental toxins. So go for seconds!

Cream your body

Make a body mask: stir 225 g/ 8 oz milk powder into 175 ml/ 6 fl oz buttermilk; stir. Spread over skin with a broad brush. Leave to dry for 15–20 minutes, then wash off with cool water.

Strawberry Collagen Cobbler

Laughter lines and crow's feet? Give your skin – and your tastebuds – a treat with this delicious strawberry dessert.

Serves 4

- 550 g/1 lb 4 oz fresh or frozen strawberries, defrosted
- 550 g/1 lb 4 oz sugar
- 350 g/12 oz plain (all-purpose) flour
- 1 tbs baking powder
- 225ml/8 fl oz/1 cup milk
- 225 g/8 oz butter, melted

1 Heat the oven to 150°C/ 300°F/Gas 2. Hull the fresh strawberries or defrost if frozen. In a blender, blitz the berries together with 225 g/ 8 oz of the sugar and 175 ml/ 6 fl oz/3/4 cup water until you have a smooth, pink purée; cover and set aside.

2 In a bowl, combine the flour with the remaining sugar, the baking powder, and the milk. Pour the melted butter into a ceramic or glass baking dish, about 23 x 33 cm/9 x 13 in. Tip in the flour mixture. Pour the strawberry purée on top of the flour mixture. Bake for 40-50 minutes in the oven.

3 Serve with a steaming cup of tea or coffee and a dollop of whipped cream if liked.

Doubtless God could have made a better berry, but doubtless God never did... (William Butler)

Strawberry fields forever... _ _

Strawberries are packed with vitamin C, vital for the formation of collagen which gives our skin strength and structure.

Strawberry tea _ _ _ _ _ _ _ _

For a strawberry infusion, steep a handful of strawberry leaves in a pot of boiling water for about 10 minutes. Drink this tisane, or leave it to cool and apply to your skin.

Peachy Skin Dessert

Here's a peachy treat that will taste of summer – and it'll also allow you to enjoy the summer sunshine without worrying about its negative effects on your skin.

Serves 4

- 4 yellow peaches
- 4 amaretto biscuits
- 1 egg yolk
- 4 tsp sugar
- 1 tbs softened butter
- Single (light) cream to serve

1 Heat the oven to 180°C/ 350°F/Gas 4. Halve the peaches and remove the stones. Create a slightly larger hollow in the peach halves so you can put more of the delicious stuffing inside.

2 In a bowl, crush the biscuits with a pestle, then combine the crumbs with the pulp you have removed from the center of the peaches, and with the egg yolk, sugar, and butter. Stir well to mix.

3 Divide the stuffing mixture between the peach halves, mounding it on top of each hollow. Grease a baking tray, place the peach halves on top, and bake in the oven for about 30 minutes. Serve with extra cream to pour over the peaches. Delicious!

The reason that the all-American boy prefers beauty to brains is that he can see better than he can think...
(Farrah Fawcett-Majors)

Forever young

The sun's UV rays cause photo-aging, which makes skin look rough, dry, and wrinkled. Luckily peaches and nectarines contain phenols, chemicals that counter-act such damage.

Beauty tip

Peaches are great for skin. At night, gently rub the fleshy side of peach peelings over your face. Leave the moisture to cleanse your skin, tighten your face muscles and prevent sagging, leaving your skin literally 'peachy'.

4

Here's Looking At You, Kid...

Find out what to eat to make yourself drop dead gorgeous...

Contents

Smiley Chicken Salad

Enjoy this delicious and low-fat main-course salad packed with vitamin B6. It produces the feel-good hormone serotonin so you can always face the world with a big smile.

Serves 4

- 1 tbs honey
- 1 tbs sherry
- 1 tbs soy sauce
- 1 chili, de-seeded and chopped
- 4 chicken breasts, boneless and skinned
- 1 head of lettuce
- 2 avocados, sliced
- 1 can (400 g/14 oz) mixed beans, drained
- 1 can (200 g/7 oz) sweetcorn (corn), drained
- Salad dressing of your choice

1 In a small bowl, combine honey, sherry, soy sauce, and chili. Brush chicken with this, cover and chill for 30 minutes.

2 Heat grill to high. Grill chicken for 15–20 minutes, turning twice, and frequently brushing with the marinade.

3 Line plates with lettuce, arrange avocado on top. Combine beans and sweetcorn (corn) and distribute on top.

4 Slice chicken breasts into strips; arrange on the salad. Drizzle with salad dressing and serve with a big smile.

Mane-Course Salad

This famous New York creation will give you glossy and silky hair so you too can shake your mane like a catwalk model.

Serves 6

- 3 egg yolks
- 2 tsp mustard
- 150 ml/¼ pint/5fl oz olive oil
- 3 tbs soured cream
- 2 tsp honey
- Salt and pepper
- 3 red apples
- 1 celeriac (celery root)
- 1 head of lettuce
- 75 g/3 oz walnut kernels
- 3 tbs lemon juice

1 In a small bowl, beat together the egg yolks and mustard. Add the oil in a thin stream, a little at a time, beating all the time. Stir in the cream and the honey, season generously to taste with salt and pepper.

2 Wash the apples, halve and core, then cut into wedges, leaving the skin on. Peel the celeriac (celery root) and cut out the 'eyes', then grate. Tear the lettuce leaves into shreds and use to line individual plates. Coarsely chop the walnut kernels.

3 Arrange the apple wedges on the lettuce and drizzle with

the lemon juice to prevent them browning. Distribute the celeriac (celery root) on top of the apple. Sprinkle with the chopped nuts. Drizzle the dressing over the top and serve.

Nutty nutrition

Nuts are a rich source of zinc, one of the minerals vital for our overall health. If your scalp is dry and flaky, eat some nuts; they'll give your hair renewed sheen and also protect against dandruff.

There is nothing that makes its way more directly to the soul than beauty...

(Joseph Addison)

Lustrous Paprika Chicken

Give your hair a protein injection and rev up its lustrous sheen. This protein-rich dinner will give you a head-turning head of hair.

Serves 4

- 2 tbs olive oil
- 4 chicken legs
- 2 onions, chopped
- 2–4 garlic cloves, crushed
- 2 red (bell) peppers, deseeded and cut into strips
- 1 tbs paprika
- Salt and pepper
- 150 ml/5 fl oz chicken stock
- 90 ml/3 fl oz low-fat yogurt
- 90 ml/3 fl oz crème fraîche

1 In a large saucepan, heat the oil and fry the chicken for about 10 minutes, turning once or twice, until browned all over. Remove chicken and set aside.

2 Add the onion and garlic and fry, stirring occasionally for about 5 minutes, or until softened. Add the paprika, stir and fry for 2 minutes. Add the (bell) peppers and cook for a further 3 minutes. Return the chicken to the saucepan, add the paprika, and season to taste with salt and pepper.

3 Pour in the stock, stir well. Bring to the boil, reduce the temperature, cover saucepan, and simmer for about 30 minutes, stirring occasionally.

4 Stir in the yogurt and crème fraîche, simmer for about 5 minutes without bringing to the boil. Check seasoning and serve on a bed of rice or ribbon noodles with a crisp side salad and a glass of beer.

Maybe it's the hair. Maybe it's the teeth. Maybe it's the intellect. No, it's the hair...
Tom Shales about Farrah Fawcett)

81

Salon protein

Protein in your diet will replenish the nutrients that are depleted by daily exposure to sun, wind, and pollution. No more split ends: this Hungarian chicken dish will give your hair body and bounce.

Good hair days

Chop 1 tsp fresh thyme, add 1 cup boiling water; steep for about 15 minutes; strain. Top up with cider vinegar to make 150 ml/5 fl oz. Add 600 ml/1 pint/20 fl oz beer. Use as a final rinse after washing your hair. Leave to dry naturally.

Beaming Broccoli Gratin

Dazzle the world with your gleaming white teeth, straight from a Hollywood film set, and benefit from the healthy nutrients of broccoli

Serves 2

- 2 tbs olive oil
- 200 g/7 oz bacon, chopped
- 1 onion, chopped
- 2 garlic cloves, crushed
- 450 g/1 lb broccoli, broken into small florets
- 200 g/7 oz mushrooms, sliced
- 200 g/7 oz blue cheese
- 425 g/15 fl oz yogurt
- 125 ml/4 fl oz milk
- 1 tbs chopped parsley

1 Heat the oven to 200°C/400°F/Gas 6. Heat 1 tbs oil in a frying pan, add the bacon, half the onion, and the garlic. Fry, stirring, for about five minutes, or until the onion is lightly browned.

2 Add the broccoli and the mushrooms, and cook over a low heat for about 5 minutes – the broccoli florets should still be crunchy. Transfer mixture to a shallow ovenproof dish.

3 Heat the second tbs of oil in the same pan, fry the other half of the onion in it, then stir in the cheese and cook over a very low heat, stirring, for 3 minutes, or until the cheese has

melted. Add the yogurt and the milk, and continue cooking, stirring all the time, for 5 minutes. Do not allow to boil. Season to taste and stir in the parsley. Pour the cheese sauce over the broccoli mixture.

4 Bake the gratin in the oven for about 20–30 minutes, or until the vegetables are done and the cheese topping is lightly browned. Serve the gratin immediately, with crusty bread and a glass of red wine.

Diets are bad for your teeth_ _

Now there's a piece of good news: dieting can be bad for you. If you often go on crash diets, your body's stores of vitamins D, B12, and calcium will plummet together with your weight, endangering your dental health. So, quickly, pass me another portion of this cheesy bake!

A smile that glow'd
celestial rosy red,
Love's proper hue...
(John Milton)

Toothsome Fruit Salad

Sore gums? The cause could be a lack of vitamin C. Save yourself a trip to the dentist and get chewing on healthy fruit.

Serves 2

- 2 egg yolks
- 50 g/2 oz sugar
- 150 g/5 oz single (light) cream
- 1 tsp vanilla sugar or a few drops vanilla essence
- 2 tbs brandy
- 1 mango
- 1 pineapple
- 4 kiwi fruit
- 1 banana
- 450 g/1 lb strawberries, hulled
- 325 g/11 oz raspberries, hulled

1 First make the brandy sauce. Beat the yolks together with the sugar until foamy. In a saucepan, bring the cream to the boil over a low heat. Stir in the vanilla sugar or essence.

2 Pour cream into egg foam, stirring. Place over boiling water. Heat, stirring, until the mixture sets.

3 Take off the heat, stir in the brandy. Pour into a cold bowl. Leave to cool; stir occasionally.

4 Meanwhile, peel the mango, remove the stone, and cut

the flesh into strips. Cut the pineapple into rings, cut off the skin and eyes, remove the central hard core, cut the flesh into chunks. Peel and slice the kiwis and the banana. Arrange all the fruit in a large bowl.

5 Pour over the chilled brandy sauce and serve.

The smile of her I love is like the dawn whose touch makes Menmon sing...
(Richard Watson Gilder)

Gleaming teeth

You can of course get your teeth professionally cleaned, bleached, contoured, and even veneered. But one of the cheapest and healthiest ways of turning your teeth into dazzling pearls is by eliminating all that stains from your diet – coffee, red wine, sugary liquids, some spices, and tobacco. For extra sweet breath, chew on a cardamom or a sprig of parsley.

Beautiful Face Bagels

A lunchtime treat to put a smile on your face – and onto the faces of all who look at you. You'll be amazed how a gleaming smile can transform any environment!

Makes 8 bagels

- 5 leaves gelatin
- ½ lemon, unwaxed or scrubbed under hot water
- 1 bunch dill
- 150 g/5 oz smoked trout or salmon
- 1 tbs crème fraîche
- 350 g/12 oz single (light) cream
- Salt and pepper
- 8 bagels

1 In a small bowl, soak the gelatin in cold water according to packet instructions. Grate the zest of the lemon, squeeze out juice. Chop dill.

2 Blitz the fish in the blender together with the crème fraîche. Stir in the dill. Squeeze out the gelatin and place in a cup over a small pan of boiling water to melt. Gently stir into the fish paste, a little at a time.

3 Beat the cream until stiff, gently fold into the fish paste. Season to taste with salt, pepper, lemon zest, and juice. Cover and chill in the fridge for 30 minutes.

4 Cut open the bagels. Stir the fish paste, then spread onto the bagel bottoms. Top with the cucumber slices, cover with the bagel tops, and serve.

The light upon her face shines from the windows of another world. Saints only have such faces...
(Henry Wadsworth Longfellow)

Bare-faced cheek _ _ _ _ _ _ _ _

Vitamin D, plentiful in trout and mackerel, hardens your teeth and helps the enamel withstand attack by food, drink and heat or cold. For a perfect smile, eat fish.

Sunny days _ _ _ _ _ _ _ _ _ _

For an extra dose of vitamin D, you need sufficient daylight, or even better, sunshine. The use of sunblocks and high SPF sun-screening products is said to have reduced our supplies of vitamin D by about 10 per cent within the last 10 years. Try to get at least 10 minutes a day in fresh air – whatever the weather.

Midnight Melon Soup

Can't quite focus on the mysterious stranger across the restaurant? Or on the road ahead as you're driving through the night? Try this fabulous chilled soup to give you perfect nighttime vision.

Serves 4

- 2 cantaloupes
- A handful fresh mint leaves
- 2 pieces preserved stem ginger in syrup, roughly chopped
- 50 g/2 oz sugar
- 1 glass orange juice
- 1 glass port
- Juice of 1/2 lemon

1 Halve the melons, remove the seeds, scoop out the flesh. Chop the mint, reserving some leaves for decoration.

2 Blitz the melon flesh and the stem ginger for a couple of seconds in the food processor until puréed but not over-processed. Add the sugar and orange juice and process again for a few seconds.

3 Stir in the mint and transfer the soup to individual serving bowls. Add a dash of port and lemon juice to taste to each bowl; stir and garnish the soup with the reserved mint leaves and serve.

People are like stained-glass windows. They sparkle and shine when the sun is out, but when the darkness sets in, their true beauty is revealed only if there is light from within... (Elizabeth Kubler Ross)

Bright eyes

Carrots and cantaloupe melons are the richest sources of beta-carotene, which the body converts into vitamin A. Vitamin A has been shown to give better vision, at night and in dim light.

Mellow melon

Puffy eyes? Drink plenty of melon juice to flush out toxins. Skin dull and lifeless? Scoop out some melon, purée, and apply to your face. Leave for 15 minutes, wash off, and moisturize. It will give your skin a healthy glow.

Bright-Eyes Squash

Enjoy this healthy, meat-free summer dish of colorful vegetables, and bring the sparkle back into your eyes.

Serves 4

- 1 large squash (spaghetti or butternut squash) or 2 small squashes (e.g. acorn squash)
- 2 tbs olive oil
- Salt and pepper
- 1 onion, chopped
- 1 garlic clove, crushed
- 1 orange (bell) pepper, de-seeded and cut into strips
- 1 green (bell) pepper, de-seeded and cut into strips
- 1 courgette (zucchini), sliced
- 1 tsp Cayenne pepper
- 1 tsp fresh rosemary leaves, chopped
- 400 g/14 oz can chopped tomatoes

1 Heat the oven to 200°C/400°F/Gas 6. Halve the squash, scoop out the seeds. Sprinkle the inside with salt and pepper, and drizzle with 1 tbs oil. Bake in the oven for 30–60 minutes, depending on thickness and variety. The squash is done when it feels soft if you insert a sharp knife into the flesh.

2 For the sauce, heat the remaining oil. Fry the onion and the garlic for 5 minutes, or

until soft. Add (bell) peppers and courgette (zucchini), cook, stirring, for about 5 minutes.

3 Stir in the Cayenne pepper and rosemary, season to taste. Add the tomatoes, stir to combine, cover and simmer over a gentle heat for about 20 minutes.

4 Pour the sauce over the squash halves and serve.

Red light for blue _ _ _ _ _ _ _

Studies have shown that lutein – in cucumbers and squash – can protect the light-sensitive areas in the retina from oxidation damage caused by harmful light.

Cool as a cucumber _ _ _ _ _ _

Cucumbers really are 11°C/20°F cooler on the inside! Revive tired or irritated eyes with two cucumber slices. Puffy eyes respond well to pads of cold, cooked potato, or cotton wool soaked in cold milk.

Marvelous Manicure Pancakes

Are your nails brittle and dry? Save yourself the visit to the beauty parlor: prepare your own ready-to-eat manicure with these super pancakes, no appointment needed.

Serves 4

- 200 g/7 oz plain (all-purpose) flour
- A pinch of salt
- 4 eggs
- 1/4 liter/9 fl oz mineral water
- 1 tbs olive oil
- 1 onion, chopped
- 1 garlic clove, crushed
- 450 g/1 lb spinach
- 1 tbs olive oil
- 1 tbs pine kernels, finely chopped
- 1 tsp sesame seeds

1 Sift flour into a large bowl, add salt, eggs, water, and whisk until you have a smooth batter. Cover and set aside for 30 minutes.

2 Meanwhile make the filling. Wash the spinach, remove thick central stems, and shred the leaves. Heat the oil in a large saucepan. Add the onion and garlic, pine kernels and sesame seeds, and fry, stirring, for 5 minutes. Add spinach; cook for 2 minutes, or until it begins to wilt.

3 Heat the oil in a large, clean frying pan. Stir batter, pour sufficient into the pan to cover base, and bake the pancakes, one at a time. Remove and keep warm in a low oven.

4 Place some of the filling on each pancake and fold. Serve immediately, with a fresh tomato salad.

I only drink to steady my nerves. Sometimes I'm so steady I don't move for months... (W. C. Fields)

Nailing the culprit

Are your nails weak, brittle, or splitting? Do they have vertical ridges? You may be suffering from calcium deficiency. Try these delicious pancakes – spinach and sesame seeds are both excellent sources of calcium and will make your nails peachy pink and perfect.

Water wonders

Drink lots of water – 2 liter/3–4 pints/1/2 gallon a day. It's good for your overall health, and in addition, it'll replenish the moisture in your fingernails.

Super Shellfish Soup

Seafood is a great all-rounder, improving all aspects of your appearance. Tuck into this divine soup and you won't need to fish for compliments.

Serves 4

- 4 dried shiitake mushrooms
- 900 ml/1½ pint/ 30 fl oz chicken stock
- 2 tbs oil
- 2 garlic cloves, crushed
- 1 piece of ginger, about 2½ cm/1 in, chopped
- 1 small chicken breast, skinned and chopped into thin strips
- 4 chilies, cut into thin rings
- 4 spring onions (scallions), cut diagonally into short lengths
- Salt and pepper

- ½ tsp sesame oil
- 50 g/2 oz crabmeat
- 25 g/1 oz fresh beansprouts
- 2 tbs lemon juice
- 1 tbs soy sauce
- 3 tbs sherry
- 1 egg

1 Soak the mushrooms for 10 minutes in hot water, squeeze out, then place in a saucepan with the stock, cover, and simmer gently over a low heat for 30 minutes.

2 Heat the oil in a frying pan, add the garlic and ginger and fry for 1 minute, stirring. Add the chicken, chilies and spring onions (scallions); fry for 5 minutes, stirring. Season, add the sesame oil, and stir. Add crabmeat and beansprouts, stir and cook for 1 minute.

3 Add stock, mushrooms, lemon juice and soy sauce to taste; stir. Simmer gently.

4 Beat the egg in a small bowl with a fork until well combined. Add the egg to the soup, stirring as it sets. Serve immediately.

Zest from zinc

Shellfish is full of zinc, perfect for toughening up brittle nails and healing inflamed skin. In addition, this miracle mineral can help delay age-related loss of vision.

Beauty is that power by which a woman charms a lover and terrifies a husband... (Ambrose Bierce)

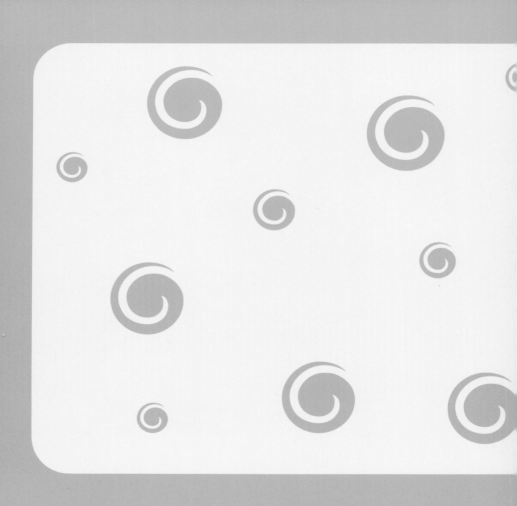